Unveiling the Homeland Security Threats of the Open US-Mexico Border Policy

Copyright Page

TITLE: Unveiling the Homeland Security Threats of the Open US-Mexico Open Border Policy

1ST Edition

Copyright @ 2023

ISBN: 9798223465089

Table of Contents

Title Page 1

Unveiling the Homeland Security Threats of the U.S.-Mexico Open Border Policy 6

Chapter 1: Introduction to Border Insecurity 7

Chapter 2: The Homeland Security Threats of the US-Mexico's Open Border Policy 13

Chapter 3: Drug Trafficking and Cartel Violence 20

Chapter 4: Human Smuggling and Trafficking 25

Chapter 5: Terrorism and Border Security 31

Chapter 6: Arms Smuggling and Illegal Firearms Trade............ 37

Chapter 7: Economic Impacts and Job Displacement 43

Chapter 8: Public Health Risks and Disease Control................ 49

Chapter 9: Environmental Concerns and Wildlife Trafficking............ 55

Chapter 10: Border Infrastructure and Management Challenges......... 61

Chapter 11: Cybersecurity Threats and Digital Crime 68

Chapter 12: Border Corruption and Organized Crime Infiltration 73

Unveiling the Homeland Security Threats of the US-Mexico Open Border Policy

By Roberto Miguel Rodriguez

Chapter 1: Introduction to Border Insecurity

The Importance of Border Security

In today's globalized world, border security has become an increasingly important issue for countries around the world. The United States has been grappling with the challenges posed by its open border policy with Mexico, and it is crucial for the public, politicians, and legislators to understand the significance of addressing these concerns. This subchapter highlights the various aspects of border security and the potential threats that arise from the US-Mexico open border policy.

One of the most pressing issues is the homeland security threats that arise due to the porous border. The unrestricted movement of people and goods across the border creates opportunities for criminals and terrorists to exploit the weaknesses in the system. Drug trafficking and cartel violence are rampant along the border, leading to increased crime rates and endangering the lives of both Americans and Mexicans.

Another consequence of the open border policy is the rise in human smuggling and trafficking. Vulnerable individuals, including women and children, are often exploited and subjected to inhumane treatment. This subchapter sheds light on the need for stringent border security measures to prevent such heinous crimes.

Terrorism is another significant concern when it comes to border security. The open border provides an avenue for potential terrorists to enter the United States undetected. This subchapter emphasizes the importance of border control in preventing terrorist activities and safeguarding national security.

Arms smuggling and the illegal firearms trade are closely linked to border security. Unregulated flow of weapons across the border contributes to the rise in crime rates and poses a threat to public safety. This subchapter discusses the need for effective border security measures to combat the illegal trade of firearms.

Additionally, the economic impacts and job displacement resulting from the open border policy cannot be overlooked. This subchapter explores the consequences of unrestricted immigration on job markets and emphasizes the need for a balanced approach to immigration policies.

Furthermore, border security is crucial for public health risks and disease control. The unregulated movement of people can lead to the spread of infectious diseases, putting the health of both Americans and Mexicans at risk. This subchapter highlights the importance of border control in protecting public health.

Environmental concerns and wildlife trafficking are also addressed in this subchapter. The open border policy creates opportunities for illegal trade in endangered species and contributes to environmental degradation. Effective border management is essential in combating such illicit activities.

Moreover, border infrastructure and management challenges, cybersecurity threats, border corruption, and organized crime infiltration are discussed to provide a comprehensive understanding of the complexities of border security.

In conclusion, this subchapter emphasizes the importance of border security in addressing the various homeland security threats posed by the US-Mexico open border policy. It aims to raise awareness among the public, politicians, and legislators about the significance of implementing effective border control measures to ensure national security, public safety, and the overall well-being of both countries.

Overview of the US-Mexico Open Border Policy

The US-Mexico open border policy has been a topic of significant concern for various stakeholders, including the public, politicians, legislators, and specialists focusing on different niches such as homeland security, drug trafficking, human smuggling, terrorism, arms smuggling, economic impacts, public health risks, environmental concerns, border infrastructure, cybersecurity, and border corruption. This subchapter aims to provide an overview of the complex issues associated with this policy and shed light on the potential threats it poses to national security and public welfare.

One of the primary concerns regarding the US-Mexico open border policy is drug trafficking and cartel violence. The vast expanse of the border, coupled with limited resources, makes it challenging to effectively intercept drug shipments and combat the violence perpetrated by drug cartels. These criminal organizations exploit the porous border to smuggle illicit drugs such as cocaine, heroin, and methamphetamine into the United States, fueling addiction rates and contributing to the rise of organized crime.

Human smuggling and trafficking are also pressing issues associated with the open border policy. Criminal networks profit from smuggling individuals across the border, often subjecting them to dangerous conditions and exploitation. This illicit trade not only endangers the lives of those being smuggled but also poses a threat to national security, as terrorists may exploit similar channels to infiltrate the country.

Arms smuggling and illegal firearms trade are additional concerns. The open border allows for the easy movement of weapons between the United States and Mexico, contributing to the violence experienced on both sides. The availability of firearms facilitates criminal activities and poses a significant challenge to law enforcement agencies.

The economic impacts of the open border policy cannot be undermined. Job displacement and wage depression in certain industries are attributed to the influx of undocumented workers. This has led to debates about the need for comprehensive immigration reform and stricter border controls to protect domestic jobs and wages.

Public health risks and disease control are also important considerations. The open border facilitates the spread of communicable diseases, posing a risk to public health. Effective disease control measures and cooperation between the two countries are imperative to mitigate these risks.

Environmental concerns arise from the unregulated movement of people and goods across the border. Wildlife trafficking, deforestation, and pollution are some of the environmental issues exacerbated by the open border policy. Collaborative efforts are required to protect the environment and preserve biodiversity.

Border infrastructure and management challenges are inherent in maintaining an open border. Developing adequate infrastructure, implementing efficient border management systems, and ensuring the proper allocation of resources are crucial for effectively managing the flow of people and goods.

The open border policy also exposes both countries to cybersecurity threats and digital crime. Criminal organizations exploit digital platforms to facilitate their operations, including money laundering and cyberattacks. Enhancing cybersecurity measures and cooperation between the United States and Mexico is essential to tackle these challenges.

Lastly, border corruption and organized crime infiltration pose significant obstacles to effective border management. The open border policy provides opportunities for corrupt officials and criminal networks to collaborate, undermining security efforts and public trust.

In conclusion, the US-Mexico open border policy presents a complex web of challenges. From drug trafficking and cartel violence to human smuggling, terrorism, arms smuggling, economic impacts, public health risks, environmental concerns, cybersecurity threats, and border corruption, these issues demand attention from policymakers, law enforcement agencies, and the public. Addressing these challenges requires a comprehensive and collaborative approach that balances security concerns with the need for efficient trade and migration.

Purpose and Significance of the Book

In today's rapidly changing world, the issue of border security has become a pressing concern for the United States. The book "Border Insecurity: Unveiling the Homeland Security Threats of the US-Mexico Open Border Policy" aims to shed light on the multifaceted challenges posed by the open border policy between the US and Mexico. This subchapter explores the purpose and significance of the book, providing an overview of the issues that will be addressed and the relevance they hold for various stakeholders, including the public, politicians, and legislators.

The primary purpose of this book is to raise awareness and foster a comprehensive understanding of the homeland security threats arising from the US-Mexico open border policy. It delves into the complex issues that emerge due to the porous nature of the border, focusing on key areas involving drug trafficking and cartel violence, human smuggling and trafficking, terrorism and border security, arms smuggling and illegal firearms trade, economic impacts and job displacement, public health risks and disease control, environmental concerns and wildlife trafficking, border infrastructure and management challenges, cybersecurity threats and digital crime, and border corruption and organized crime infiltration.

By addressing these topics, the book aims to equip the public with the knowledge needed to engage in informed discussions and make sound decisions on border security. It also serves as a wake-up call for politicians and legislators, urging them to prioritize and take necessary actions to safeguard national security interests. The implications of an insecure border extend far beyond the immediate homeland security concerns. They affect the economy, public health, the environment, and even the digital realm, making it imperative for policymakers to develop effective strategies to mitigate these threats.

Furthermore, the book caters to specific niches within the broader audience. It provides valuable insights for those interested in understanding the homeland security threats of the US-Mexico open border policy. Individuals concerned about drug trafficking and cartel violence, human smuggling and trafficking, terrorism, arms smuggling, economic impacts, public health risks, environmental concerns, border infrastructure and management challenges, cybersecurity threats, and border corruption will find this book to be a valuable resource.

In conclusion, "Border Insecurity: Unveiling the Homeland Security Threats of the US-Mexico Open Border Policy" serves as a comprehensive guide that explores the various dimensions of the open border policy. By examining the implications of an insecure border, the book aims to inform and engage the public, politicians, legislators, and individuals interested in the diverse range of homeland security threats associated with the US-Mexico border.

Chapter 2: The Homeland Security Threats of the US-Mexico's Open Border Policy

Border Infiltration by Criminal Organizations

Introduction:

The US-Mexico open border policy has been a subject of intense debate, with proponents citing economic benefits and humanitarian concerns, while opponents highlight the security threats posed by criminal organizations. This subchapter aims to shed light on the issue of border infiltration by criminal organizations, outlining the dangers they pose to the homeland security of the United States.

The Scope of the Problem:

Criminal organizations, such as drug cartels and human smugglers, have taken advantage of the porosity of the US-Mexico border to infiltrate the country. They exploit weak spots in border security to transport drugs, weapons, and people illegally into the United States. This infiltration poses a significant threat to the safety and well-being of American citizens.

Drug Trafficking and Cartel Violence:

The open border policy has inadvertently facilitated the growth of drug trafficking across the US-Mexico border. Criminal organizations utilize sophisticated tactics and technology to smuggle drugs into the United States, leading to an increase in cartel violence and drug-related crimes. This poses a direct threat to public safety and national security.

Human Smuggling and Trafficking:

Criminal organizations involved in human smuggling and trafficking exploit vulnerable individuals seeking a better life in America. They subject them to inhumane conditions, endangering their lives and violating their basic human rights. The lack of effective border control measures allows these criminal organizations to continue their illicit operations, highlighting the urgent need for enhanced security and immigration reform.

Terrorism and Border Security:

The porous border also raises concerns regarding terrorism. While the majority of unauthorized border crossings are motivated by economic reasons, the potential for terrorists to exploit the open border cannot be ignored. Proper border security measures are essential to prevent the infiltration of terrorist elements who may seek to carry out attacks on US soil.

Arms Smuggling and Illegal Firearms Trade:

Criminal organizations exploit the open border to smuggle firearms and weapons illegally into the United States, contributing to the rising rates of gun violence. The ease with which illegal firearms can be brought across the border poses a grave threat to public safety and necessitates stricter border control measures.

Conclusion:

The infiltration of criminal organizations across the US-Mexico border poses a significant threat to the homeland security of the United States. Drug trafficking, cartel violence, human smuggling, terrorism, arms smuggling, and other illicit activities thrive due to the porous nature of the border. Addressing these challenges requires a comprehensive approach, including enhanced border security, immigration reforms, and international cooperation. The safety and well-being of American citizens should be prioritized, while also ensuring that any policy changes effectively balance security concerns with humanitarian considerations. By addressing the issue of border infiltration by criminal organizations, the United States can take a crucial step towards securing its borders and safeguarding the welfare of its people.

Smuggling Routes and Criminal Networks

Introduction:

In this subchapter, we will delve into the alarming issue of smuggling routes and criminal networks operating along the US-Mexico border. The illicit activities conducted by these criminal elements pose significant threats to homeland security, public safety, and national interests. By understanding the intricacies of smuggling routes and criminal networks, we can shed light on the urgent need for effective border security measures to combat these threats.

1. The homeland security threats of the US-Mexico's open border policy:

The open border policy between the US and Mexico has inadvertently facilitated the growth of smuggling routes and criminal networks. This chapter will explore how this policy has enabled the unchecked movement of contraband, including drugs, weapons, and human trafficking, thereby endangering national security.

2. Drug trafficking and cartel violence:

The US-Mexico border has become a hotbed for drug trafficking, with powerful cartels exploiting smuggling routes to transport narcotics into the United States. We will examine the extent of this issue and the resulting violence that plagues both sides of the border, necessitating a comprehensive border security strategy.

3. Human smuggling and trafficking:

Criminal networks have capitalized on the open border to engage in human smuggling and trafficking activities. This subchapter will explore the shocking realities faced by migrants as they are exploited and subjected to inhumane conditions during their journey. We will also highlight the need for improved border security measures to protect vulnerable individuals.

4. Terrorism and border security:

The porous US-Mexico border poses a potential threat for terrorist organizations seeking entry into the United States. We will discuss the challenges faced by border security agencies in preventing the infiltration of these elements and the importance of bolstering border security to mitigate this risk.

5. Arms smuggling and illegal firearms trade:

Smuggling routes provide an avenue for the illegal trade of firearms, contributing to the proliferation of weapons in both countries. This section will analyze the implications of arms smuggling on public safety and the need for stricter border control measures to curb this dangerous trend.

Conclusion:

In this subchapter, we have examined the various facets of smuggling routes and criminal networks that thrive along the US-Mexico border. We have highlighted the grave homeland security threats posed by drug trafficking, human smuggling, terrorism, arms smuggling, and other illicit activities. By recognizing these challenges, it becomes evident that immediate action is required to enhance border security measures, protect public safety, and safeguard national interests. The adoption of a comprehensive and robust border security policy is essential to address these pressing issues and ensure a secure and prosperous future for both the United States and Mexico.

Impact on National Security and Public Safety

The US-Mexico open border policy has far-reaching implications for both national security and public safety. This subchapter delves into the various ways in which this policy impacts these crucial aspects of our society, shedding light on the urgent need for comprehensive border security measures.

One of the most significant threats posed by the open border policy is the proliferation of drug trafficking and cartel violence. The porous border allows drug cartels to smuggle vast quantities of illicit drugs into the United States, fueling addiction and contributing to crime rates. The violence stemming from territorial disputes between rival cartels spills over into American cities, endangering the lives of innocent civilians.

Another pressing concern is human smuggling and trafficking, which thrives in the absence of strict border controls. Vulnerable individuals, including women and children, are exploited and subjected to unimaginable hardships as they are smuggled across the border. This illicit trade not only puts lives at risk but also undermines our commitment to human rights.

Terrorism also poses a grave threat to national security, and the open border policy provides an avenue for potential terrorists to infiltrate our country undetected. With the rise of global terrorism, it is imperative that we secure our borders to prevent any potential threats from entering our nation.

Arms smuggling and the illegal firearms trade are further consequences of an open border. Criminal organizations take advantage of the lax security measures to traffic weapons, contributing to the proliferation of illegal firearms in our communities. This poses a significant risk to public safety, as these weapons are often used in violent crimes.

The economic impacts of the open border policy cannot be overlooked. Job displacement is a growing concern as undocumented immigrants often compete with American workers for employment opportunities. This not only affects job availability but also puts downward pressure on wages, leading to economic instability.

Public health risks and disease control are also compromised by the lack of border security. The influx of individuals with undocumented health conditions poses a risk to public health, potentially leading to the spread of infectious diseases.

Environmental concerns are another consequence of an unsecured border. Wildlife trafficking, deforestation, and other illegal activities have a detrimental impact on the environment, disrupting delicate ecosystems and endangering endangered species.

Border infrastructure and management challenges are significant hurdles in ensuring effective border security. The strain on existing resources, including personnel and technology, hampers our ability to effectively monitor and control the flow of goods and individuals across the border.

Furthermore, the digital age has brought about new threats, with cybersecurity threats and digital crime becoming increasingly prevalent. Our open border policy provides opportunities for cybercriminals to exploit vulnerabilities in our digital infrastructure, posing a threat to national security.

Lastly, border corruption and organized crime infiltration are persistent challenges that undermine our efforts to maintain national security. The open border policy can facilitate the infiltration of criminal organizations and corrupt officials, further exacerbating existing security risks.

In conclusion, the US-Mexico open border policy has wide-ranging implications for national security and public safety. From drug trafficking and cartel violence to terrorism and cybersecurity threats, it is imperative that we address these issues through comprehensive border security measures. By doing so, we can safeguard our communities, protect our citizens, and ensure a safer and more secure future for all.

Chapter 3: Drug Trafficking and Cartel Violence

Overview of Drug Trafficking Organizations

Drug trafficking organizations (DTOs) are sophisticated criminal networks that play a significant role in the global illegal drug trade. This subchapter aims to provide an overview of these organizations and their impact on the United States-Mexico border, shedding light on the alarming homeland security threats posed by the open border policy.

DTOs operate as transnational criminal enterprises, smuggling illicit drugs across the border and distributing them throughout the United States. These organizations are highly organized and possess extensive resources, allowing them to adapt to law enforcement efforts and exploit vulnerabilities in border security. Their activities not only fuel drug addiction and contribute to societal deterioration but also generate substantial profits that are often used to fund other criminal activities, including terrorism.

The drug trafficking and cartel violence stemming from these organizations have plagued both sides of the border. The intense competition and territorial disputes among rival cartels have resulted in a surge of violence, leading to widespread fear and instability in the region. The public, politicians, and legislators must understand the gravity of this issue and the urgent need for comprehensive border security measures.

Furthermore, the involvement of DTOs in human smuggling and trafficking further exacerbates the situation. These organizations exploit vulnerable individuals, often subjecting them to inhumane conditions and violence. The open border policy provides an avenue for DTOs to engage in these illicit activities, posing a significant threat to national security and human rights.

The influence of DTOs extends beyond drug and human trafficking to the smuggling of illegal firearms and arms trade. The porous border allows for the easy flow of weapons into the United States, contributing to the proliferation of violence and endangering the lives of citizens. The chapter will delve into the interconnectedness of arms smuggling, drug trafficking, and terrorism, emphasizing the need for robust border security measures to mitigate these threats.

In addition to the security risks, drug trafficking organizations have severe economic impacts, leading to job displacement and draining resources from local communities. The public health risks associated with drug addiction, disease control challenges, and environmental concerns such as wildlife trafficking further highlight the need to address these issues comprehensively.

This chapter will also shed light on the challenges faced in border infrastructure and management, emphasizing the need for investment in technology, personnel, and logistical resources to counter DTOs effectively. Additionally, the increasing cybersecurity threats and digital crimes associated with DTOs' operations and their infiltration into border corruption and organized crime cannot be overlooked.

It is imperative that the public, politicians, and legislators understand the multifaceted nature of drug trafficking organizations and their detrimental effects on society. Only through a holistic understanding of these issues can we work towards implementing effective policies and enhancing border security measures to combat the threats posed by DTOs and protect the interests of the nation.

Routes and Methods of Drug Trafficking

Drug trafficking is a significant problem that continues to pose a serious threat to the security and well-being of the United States. Understanding the routes and methods used by drug traffickers is crucial in developing effective strategies to combat this illicit activity. In this subchapter, we will delve into the various routes and methods employed by drug traffickers, shedding light on the complexity and scale of this issue.

One of the primary routes used by drug traffickers is the US-Mexico border. The vast, porous border spanning thousands of miles provides an ideal gateway for smuggling drugs into the United States. Traffickers exploit the numerous points of entry, including legal ports of entry, remote areas, and underground tunnels. These routes are preferred due to their proximity to drug production regions in South and Central America.

Air transportation is another common method employed by drug traffickers. Small aircraft and private planes are used to smuggle drugs across the border, often landing in remote areas or makeshift airstrips. Traffickers also utilize commercial airlines, hiding drugs within luggage or even inside the bodies of couriers known as "mules." The use of drones has also emerged as a new and concerning trend in drug trafficking, allowing traffickers to bypass traditional border security measures.

Maritime routes are extensively exploited by drug cartels as well. Vast stretches of coastline along the US-Mexico border provide ample opportunities for drug smugglers to transport large quantities of drugs by sea. Fishing boats, pleasure crafts, and cargo ships are used to conceal and transport drugs, often transferring them to smaller vessels that can easily evade detection.

In addition to these traditional methods, drug traffickers have embraced technology to facilitate their operations. The dark web and encrypted communication platforms allow for the anonymous sale and distribution of drugs, making it difficult for law enforcement agencies to track and apprehend traffickers. Cryptocurrencies, such as Bitcoin, are also used in drug transactions, further complicating efforts to disrupt the flow of drugs.

Understanding these routes and methods is crucial in developing comprehensive strategies to combat drug trafficking. It requires collaboration between law enforcement agencies, intelligence agencies, and international partners to dismantle the sophisticated networks that facilitate this illicit trade. By investing in border security infrastructure, leveraging technology, and enhancing intelligence sharing, we can make significant strides in disrupting the drug trade and safeguarding our communities.

As public awareness and concern about drug trafficking grow, it is imperative for politicians and legislators to prioritize the issue and allocate resources to address it effectively. By doing so, we can protect our borders, communities, and the well-being of our nation as a whole.

Rise of Cartel Violence and its Consequences

In recent years, the United States has witnessed a disturbing surge in cartel violence along its porous border with Mexico. This rise in violence is a direct consequence of the flawed open border policy that has been in place, and it poses grave threats to the homeland security of both nations. This subchapter aims to shed light on the extent of the problem and highlight its far-reaching consequences.

Drug trafficking and cartel violence go hand in hand, with the cartels using their brutal tactics to maintain control over the lucrative drug trade. These criminal organizations have established a web of corruption, intimidation, and violence that stretches across both sides of the border. The consequences of their actions are felt not only in terms of lives lost but also in the destabilization of communities, as cartels infiltrate local institutions and exploit vulnerable populations.

The impact of cartel violence is not limited to drug trafficking alone. It extends to other illicit activities such as human smuggling and trafficking, terrorism, arms smuggling, economic disruptions, public health risks, environmental concerns, cybersecurity, and border corruption. Each of these areas presents unique challenges that demand immediate attention from policymakers and legislators.

From an economic standpoint, the rise of cartel violence has led to job displacement and economic instability in border communities. The constant threat of violence and the perception of an unsafe border deter investment and stifle economic growth. Moreover, the illegal arms trade facilitated by these criminal organizations poses a significant risk to public safety, as firearms flow freely across the border, fueling violence on both sides.

The consequences of cartel violence also extend to public health risks, as drug trafficking routes become conduits for the spread of diseases. Furthermore, the environmental impact of cartel activities cannot be overlooked, with wildlife trafficking and habitat destruction taking a toll on fragile ecosystems.

Addressing the rise of cartel violence requires a comprehensive approach, encompassing border infrastructure and management challenges, enhanced cybersecurity measures, and a crackdown on corruption. Only by recognizing the interconnectedness of these threats can we hope to develop effective strategies to combat them.

It is imperative that the public, politicians, and legislators acknowledge the gravity of the situation and work together to implement robust policies to secure the border and counter the influence of cartels. Failure to do so will not only perpetuate the violence but also expose the nation to increased homeland security threats. The time for action is now.

Chapter 4: Human Smuggling and Trafficking

Human Smuggling Networks and Routes

Human smuggling is a grave concern that arises due to the porous nature of the US-Mexico border. This subchapter aims to shed light on the intricate networks and routes employed by human smugglers, and the associated risks and consequences. It is essential for the public, politicians, and legislators to understand the extent of this issue and its impact on various aspects of society.

Human smuggling is a profitable criminal enterprise, with smugglers exploiting vulnerable individuals seeking a better life or fleeing from dire circumstances. These smugglers operate highly organized networks, employing various routes to transport migrants across the border undetected. These routes span the vast expanse of the border, including remote desert areas, river crossings, and even tunnels. Smugglers utilize a range of methods, such as stashing individuals in hidden compartments within vehicles or guiding them through treacherous terrain under cover of darkness.

The implications of human smuggling extend beyond mere immigration concerns. Firstly, it poses significant humanitarian risks, as migrants often face perilous conditions during their journey. Many have lost their lives due to dehydration, suffocation in cramped vehicles, or exposure to extreme weather conditions. The exploitation and abuse of migrants by smugglers further exacerbate this humanitarian crisis.

Moreover, human smuggling serves as a facilitator for other illicit activities, including drug trafficking and terrorism. The same networks that smuggle people across the border also provide opportunities for drug cartels and terrorist organizations to infiltrate the United States.

This intertwining of criminal activities poses a direct threat to national security, demanding immediate attention from policymakers and law enforcement agencies.

Furthermore, the economic impacts of human smuggling cannot be overlooked. Job displacement and unfair labor practices create significant challenges for both American citizens and legal immigrants, affecting wages and job opportunities. Additionally, public health risks arise due to the potential spread of diseases carried by migrants, highlighting the need for robust disease control measures.

The environmental concerns associated with human smuggling also merit attention. The smuggling routes often traverse delicate ecosystems, leading to environmental degradation. Wildlife trafficking is also facilitated by these networks, endangering various species and disrupting ecological balance.

Addressing the challenges posed by human smuggling requires comprehensive border infrastructure and management. Enhancing border security measures, including technology and personnel, is crucial to curb these illicit activities. Additionally, policymakers must prioritize international cooperation and information sharing to dismantle the transnational networks behind human smuggling.

In conclusion, human smuggling networks and routes present a multifaceted challenge to homeland security. By understanding the extent of this issue and its interconnectedness with other threats, the public, politicians, and legislators can work together to develop effective strategies to combat human smuggling and protect the nation's interests. It is imperative that all stakeholders prioritize the security, welfare, and prosperity of the United States and its citizens.

Exploitation and Trafficking of Vulnerable Individuals

Introduction:

The exploitation and trafficking of vulnerable individuals is a grave issue that demands immediate attention in the context of the US-Mexico open border policy. This subchapter aims to shed light on the distressing reality faced by countless individuals who fall victim to human smuggling and trafficking. By understanding the magnitude of this problem, we can strengthen our resolve to address it effectively.

Understanding the Issue:

Human smuggling and trafficking represent a multi-billion dollar industry that preys on the most vulnerable populations, including women, children, and migrants seeking a better life. Traffickers exploit their desperation, luring them into dangerous situations where they become victims of physical and psychological abuse. The lack of effective border security measures exacerbates this problem, allowing criminal networks to operate with relative ease.

Consequences and Implications:

The consequences of trafficking and exploitation are far-reaching. Not only do the victims suffer immediate harm, but the societal impact is profound. The public health risks associated with insufficient disease control, the economic impacts of job displacement, and the environmental concerns stemming from wildlife trafficking are just a few of the implications of this crisis. Additionally, the infiltration of organized crime and corruption within border security further exacerbates this issue, posing a direct threat to national security.

Call to Action:

It is imperative that the public, politicians, and legislators come together to address this critical issue. Strengthening border security measures, increasing funding for law enforcement agencies, and enhancing international cooperation are crucial steps in combating human smuggling and trafficking. Furthermore, developing comprehensive support systems for victims and prioritizing the prosecution of traffickers will provide much-needed relief to those affected.

Conclusion:

The exploitation and trafficking of vulnerable individuals is a dark reality that cannot be ignored. By understanding the complex dynamics involved, we can work towards implementing effective solutions. It is only through a collective effort that we can ensure the safety and well-being of those who are most at risk. The time to act is now; let us work together to dismantle the networks that perpetuate this heinous crime and provide a safer future for all.

Impacts on Human Rights and Public Safety

The US-Mexico open border policy has significant impacts on human rights and public safety, which cannot be ignored. This subchapter aims to shed light on the various consequences that arise from this policy, impacting the lives of individuals and the overall security of both nations.

One of the most pressing concerns is the rampant drug trafficking and cartel violence that plagues the border region. The open border policy inadvertently facilitates the movement of drugs across the border, leading to a surge in drug-related crimes and violence. Innocent lives are lost, families are torn apart, and communities suffer as a result of the drug trade.

Moreover, human smuggling and trafficking are grave human rights violations that are intricately tied to the open border policy. Vulnerable individuals seeking a better life are often exploited by criminal networks, leading to their abuse and enslavement. This not only violates their basic human rights but also poses a significant threat to public safety.

Terrorism and border security are also major concerns. The open border policy can potentially allow terrorists to enter the United States undetected, posing a grave threat to national security. It is crucial to implement robust border security measures to prevent the infiltration of terrorist organizations and protect the public from acts of terror.

Arms smuggling and the illegal firearms trade are additional consequences of the open border policy. Criminals take advantage of the porous border to traffic weapons illegally, exacerbating the already alarming rates of gun violence in both nations. This poses a direct threat to public safety and necessitates stricter border control measures.

Economic impacts and job displacement are also significant factors to consider. The open border policy can result in job displacement for American citizens due to the influx of undocumented workers. This creates economic instability and affects the livelihoods of individuals, leading to social unrest and discontent among the public.

Public health risks and disease control are vital concerns in the open border region. The unrestricted movement of individuals can contribute to the spread of infectious diseases, posing a threat to public health. Proper disease control measures and healthcare infrastructure are essential to mitigate these risks.

Environmental concerns and wildlife trafficking are intertwined with the open border policy. The unchecked movement of individuals and goods can lead to environmental degradation and the illegal trade of endangered wildlife, threatening biodiversity and disrupting ecosystems.

Border infrastructure and management challenges also emerge as a consequence of the open border policy. There is a need for better infrastructure and management systems to ensure efficient border control and address the security concerns mentioned above.

Finally, cybersecurity threats and digital crimes cannot be overlooked. The open border policy can provide opportunities for cybercriminals to exploit vulnerabilities in the digital infrastructure, compromising public safety and national security.

Addressing these impacts on human rights and public safety requires a comprehensive approach that involves collaboration between the United States and Mexico. Stricter border control measures, improved law enforcement cooperation, and enhanced international partnerships are essential to mitigate these threats effectively. It is imperative for politicians, legislators, and the public to acknowledge these challenges and work towards sustainable solutions that prioritize human rights and ensure public safety.

Chapter 5: Terrorism and Border Security

Potential for Terrorist Infiltration

One of the most critical aspects of border security that demands immediate attention is the potential for terrorist infiltration. While the US-Mexico open border policy may have its benefits, it also presents significant risks that must not be ignored. This subchapter aims to shed light on the alarming threats posed by terrorists exploiting the porous border, emphasizing the urgency for heightened security measures.

Terrorist organizations, such as ISIS and Al-Qaeda, have repeatedly expressed their intent to exploit weak border controls to infiltrate the United States. The vast expanse of the US-Mexico border, stretching over 1,900 miles, provides an ideal entry point for these extremists to smuggle themselves and their weapons into the country. This poses an immediate danger to the safety and security of the American public.

The open border policy inadvertently aids terrorists in their efforts to establish sleeper cells and plan attacks within the United States. The lack of proper screening and surveillance mechanisms allows these individuals to blend seamlessly with the flow of migrants, making it challenging for law enforcement agencies to identify and apprehend them. This vulnerability puts the country at an increased risk of large-scale terrorist attacks, similar to those witnessed in Europe and other parts of the world.

To effectively address this threat, it is imperative for politicians, legislators, and the public to acknowledge the urgent need for comprehensive border security reforms. This includes increasing the number of border patrol agents, deploying advanced surveillance technologies, and enhancing intelligence sharing and cooperation between federal, state, and local law enforcement agencies.

Moreover, collaboration with international partners is crucial to disrupt transnational terrorist networks and prevent them from exploiting the US-Mexico border. Strengthening intelligence sharing and joint operations with countries facing similar challenges will contribute to a more robust defense against terrorist infiltration.

By prioritizing the security of our borders, we not only protect our citizens but also send a strong message to terrorist organizations that their attempts to exploit our vulnerabilities will not go unanswered. It is the responsibility of our leaders and policymakers to implement effective border security measures that strike a balance between facilitating legitimate trade and travel while ensuring the safety and security of our nation.

In conclusion, the potential for terrorist infiltration through the US-Mexico border is a pressing issue that demands immediate attention. By addressing this threat, we safeguard the well-being of the American public and send a clear message that our borders are secure. It is imperative for politicians, legislators, and the public to understand the gravity of this issue and take decisive action to protect our homeland.

Border Security Measures to Counter Terrorism

In recent years, the issue of border security has become a pressing concern for many countries, especially those sharing borders with regions plagued by terrorism. The United States, in particular, has faced numerous challenges in securing its border with Mexico, which has been a hotbed for various homeland security threats. This subchapter aims to explore the border security measures that can effectively counter terrorism and mitigate the risks associated with the US-Mexico open border policy.

Terrorism poses a significant threat to national security, and it is crucial to implement robust border security measures to prevent the infiltration of terrorists and the smuggling of weapons and explosives. The first step towards enhancing border security is to establish a comprehensive surveillance system that includes advanced technologies such as drones, surveillance cameras, and sensors. These tools can provide real-time monitoring of border areas, enabling law enforcement agencies to detect and respond to any suspicious activities promptly.

In addition to surveillance, increasing the number of border patrol agents is essential. These agents should be adequately trained and equipped with the necessary resources to effectively detect, apprehend, and deter terrorists attempting to cross the border. Collaboration between different agencies, such as the Department of Homeland Security, Customs and Border Protection, and local law enforcement, is also crucial in sharing intelligence and coordinating efforts to combat terrorism.

Moreover, intelligence gathering and analysis play a vital role in countering terrorism at the border. Strengthening partnerships with international intelligence agencies and improving information sharing can help identify potential threats and disrupt terrorist networks. Implementing a robust visa screening process and enhancing the collection and analysis of biometric data can further enhance border security and prevent the entry of individuals with known terrorist ties.

Another crucial aspect of border security is the development of strong border infrastructure. This includes the construction of physical barriers in high-risk areas and upgrading existing infrastructure to prevent unauthorized border crossings. Furthermore, investing in advanced technology and equipment, such as non-intrusive inspection systems and radiation detectors, can improve the detection of hidden contraband and weapons.

Lastly, public awareness and engagement are vital in combating terrorism at the border. Educating the public about the risks associated with open borders and the importance of reporting suspicious activities can help create a vigilant society. Politicians and legislators must also prioritize border security and allocate sufficient resources to enhance security measures.

In conclusion, countering terrorism requires a multi-faceted approach, and border security measures play a crucial role in mitigating the risks associated with the US-Mexico open border policy. By investing in surveillance technologies, increasing border patrol agents, improving intelligence gathering and analysis, developing strong border infrastructure, and promoting public awareness, the United States can effectively counter terrorism and safeguard its national security.

Collaboration with International Partners

In order to effectively address the myriad of challenges posed by the US-Mexico open border policy, collaboration with international partners is crucial. The threats of drug trafficking, cartel violence, human smuggling and trafficking, terrorism, arms smuggling, economic impacts, public health risks, environmental concerns, border infrastructure challenges, cybersecurity threats, and border corruption cannot be overcome by one country alone. It requires the collective efforts of multiple nations working together towards a common goal of preserving homeland security.

International collaboration is vital when it comes to combating drug trafficking and cartel violence. Drug cartels operate across borders, making it essential for countries to exchange intelligence, share resources, and coordinate efforts to disrupt their operations. By collaborating with international partners, law enforcement agencies can enhance their capabilities to track and dismantle these criminal networks, ultimately reducing the flow of illicit drugs into our communities.

Similarly, the issue of human smuggling and trafficking requires international cooperation. Trafficking networks span multiple countries, and victims often originate from different nations. By working together, countries can pool their resources to dismantle these networks, rescue victims, and prosecute the perpetrators. International collaboration can also lead to the development of comprehensive strategies to address the root causes of human smuggling and trafficking, such as poverty and lack of opportunities, thereby preventing future incidents.

The threat of terrorism and border security is another area where collaboration with international partners is paramount. Terrorist organizations have proven to be highly adaptable, exploiting weak border controls and using cross-border movements to carry out their activities. By sharing intelligence, coordinating border surveillance efforts, and implementing joint counter-terrorism operations, countries can enhance their ability to detect and prevent terrorist activities.

Arms smuggling and illegal firearms trade also require international collaboration. Criminal organizations exploit porous borders to traffic arms, fueling violence and instability. By working together, countries can strengthen border controls, implement stricter regulations on arms sales, and enhance information sharing to disrupt these illegal activities.

Additionally, collaboration with international partners is crucial when it comes to addressing economic impacts, public health risks, environmental concerns, border infrastructure challenges, cybersecurity threats, and border corruption. These issues transcend national boundaries and require a coordinated response to mitigate their effects.

In conclusion, the challenges posed by the US-Mexico open border policy necessitate collaboration with international partners. By working together, countries can enhance their collective ability to combat drug trafficking, cartel violence, human smuggling, terrorism, arms smuggling, economic impacts, public health risks, environmental concerns, border infrastructure challenges, cybersecurity threats, and border corruption. It is only through international collaboration that we can secure our borders and safeguard our communities, economies, and the well-being of our citizens.

Chapter 6: Arms Smuggling and Illegal Firearms Trade

Overview of Arms Smuggling Activities

Arms smuggling and the illegal firearms trade have become significant concerns in the context of the US-Mexico open border policy. This subchapter aims to provide an overview of the activities associated with arms smuggling, shedding light on the impact it has on homeland security, public safety, and the overall well-being of the nation.

Arms smuggling refers to the illegal transportation and trade of firearms across international borders. The US-Mexico border has been a hotspot for such activities, with an alarming number of firearms flowing from the United States into Mexico. These weapons often end up in the hands of drug cartels, criminal organizations, and other nefarious actors, fueling violence, crime, and instability in both countries.

The porous nature of the US-Mexico border, coupled with the high demand for weapons in Mexico, has made it a lucrative market for arms smugglers. Criminal networks exploit various methods to transport firearms, including hidden compartments in vehicles, tunnels, and even drones. Moreover, the vast expanse of the border and the limited resources available for monitoring and enforcement pose significant challenges for law enforcement agencies.

The consequences of arms smuggling are far-reaching. The availability of illegal firearms contributes to the intensification of drug trafficking and cartel violence, as these groups utilize firearms to protect their territories and engage in armed confrontations. This, in turn, poses a threat to public safety, not only in border regions but also throughout the entire country.

Additionally, the proliferation of illegal firearms increases the risk of terrorism and compromises border security. Terrorist organizations may exploit the open border policy to smuggle weapons and potentially carry out attacks on US soil. The absence of stringent checks and controls at the border facilitates the movement of dangerous individuals and weapons, undermining national security.

Moreover, the economic impacts of arms smuggling cannot be ignored. The prevalence of violence and insecurity deters foreign investment, hampers economic development, and results in job displacement in border regions. The negative consequences extend beyond the immediate security concerns, affecting the livelihoods and well-being of communities on both sides of the border.

It is crucial for policymakers, legislators, and the public to understand the gravity of arms smuggling and its implications. By addressing this issue, strengthening border infrastructure and management, enhancing cooperation between law enforcement agencies, and implementing stricter firearm regulations, we can mitigate the threats posed by illegal firearms trade and safeguard the security and well-being of our nation.

Impact on Crime Rates and Public Safety

The issue of crime rates and public safety is a major concern when discussing the impact of the US-Mexico open border policy. Understanding the magnitude of the problem is crucial for the public, politicians, and legislators alike.

One of the most significant consequences of the open border policy is the rise in drug trafficking and cartel violence. The porous border allows for an influx of illegal drugs, resulting in an increase in addiction rates and drug-related crimes. The cartels take advantage of the unregulated border to transport drugs, leading to violence and territorial disputes. This poses a direct threat to the safety of both US and Mexican citizens.

Another grave concern is human smuggling and trafficking. The open border policy facilitates the movement of individuals across the border, making it easier for human smugglers and traffickers to operate. This leads to exploitation, forced labor, and sex trafficking. The safety of vulnerable individuals, including women and children, is compromised due to the lack of effective border control.

Terrorism is another issue that arises from the open border policy. The unrestricted movement of people and goods provides an opportunity for potential terrorists to enter the United States undetected. This poses a significant national security threat and can have severe consequences for public safety.

Arms smuggling and the illegal firearms trade are also facilitated by the open border policy. Criminals take advantage of the porous border to smuggle firearms into the United States, fueling the already alarming rates of gun violence. This poses a direct threat to public safety as these weapons end up in the hands of criminals.

In addition to the direct impact on crime rates, the open border policy also has economic implications. Job displacement is a significant concern as illegal immigrants often take low-wage jobs, leading to unemployment and wage depression among the local population. This can lead to socioeconomic tensions and increased crime rates.

Public health risks and disease control are also compromised due to the open border policy. The lack of proper screening and control measures allows for the spread of infectious diseases. This poses a risk not only to border communities but also to the entire nation.

Environmental concerns and wildlife trafficking are additional consequences of the open border policy. Unregulated border crossings can lead to environmental degradation, habitat destruction, and an increase in wildlife trafficking. This poses a threat to biodiversity and the delicate ecosystems along the border.

Border infrastructure and management challenges are also significant issues. The open border policy puts a strain on existing resources, making it difficult to effectively manage and secure the border. This further exacerbates the crime rates and compromises public safety.

The open border policy also opens the door to cybersecurity threats and digital crime. Criminal organizations can exploit vulnerabilities in digital systems, compromising sensitive information and posing a threat to national security.

Lastly, the infiltration of organized crime and corruption is a significant problem resulting from the open border policy. Criminal organizations take advantage of the weak border control to infiltrate institutions and engage in corruption, further compromising public safety.

In conclusion, the impact of the US-Mexico open border policy on crime rates and public safety is profound. Drug trafficking, human smuggling, terrorism, arms smuggling, economic implications, public health risks, environmental concerns, border infrastructure challenges, cybersecurity threats, and organized crime infiltration are all consequences that need to be addressed urgently. It is crucial for the public, politicians, and legislators to understand the gravity of these issues and work towards implementing effective policies to ensure the safety and security of both nations.

Efforts to Combat Arms Smuggling and Trade

Arms smuggling and the illegal firearms trade pose significant threats to the security of both the United States and Mexico. To address this grave concern, concerted efforts have been made by both countries to combat the illicit movement of weapons across the border. This subchapter highlights the various initiatives and strategies employed to tackle arms smuggling and trade.

Recognizing the need for enhanced cooperation, the United States and Mexico have collaborated extensively in sharing intelligence, conducting joint operations, and implementing stricter border control measures. The U.S. Department of Homeland Security and its Mexican counterparts have established task forces and specialized units to specifically target arms trafficking networks. These units focus on disrupting the supply chains, identifying the sources of illicit firearms, and apprehending the individuals involved in this criminal activity.

One of the key initiatives in combating arms smuggling is the implementation of advanced technology and equipment at border crossings. X-ray scanners, firearms tracing systems, and other sophisticated tools have been deployed to detect hidden weapons and identify their origins. Moreover, the use of biometric technology has improved the accuracy of identifying individuals involved in arms smuggling.

To deter the illegal trade of firearms, both countries have strengthened their legislative frameworks. Stricter penalties for arms trafficking have been put in place, including longer prison sentences and heavier fines. Additionally, efforts have been made to improve the tracking and registration of firearms, ensuring that legal weapons do not end up in the hands of criminals.

International cooperation has also been vital in combating arms smuggling. The United States and Mexico have engaged with other countries, particularly those in Central and South America, to share best practices, coordinate efforts, and exchange information on arms trafficking networks that operate across borders.

While significant progress has been made, challenges remain in addressing arms smuggling and trade comprehensively. These challenges include the vastness of the border, limited resources, corruption, and the sheer volume of illegal firearms already in circulation. Therefore, continued investment in intelligence sharing, technology, and personnel training is necessary to effectively combat this threat.

By addressing arms smuggling and trade head-on, the United States and Mexico are taking vital steps towards enhancing border security and safeguarding their citizens. However, the fight against arms trafficking is an ongoing battle that requires sustained commitment, collaboration, and innovative strategies to stay one step ahead of the criminals who seek to exploit the open border policy.

Chapter 7: Economic Impacts and Job Displacement

Effects of Illegal Immigration on the Economy

Introduction:

Illegal immigration has long been a contentious issue, particularly in countries with porous borders like the United States and Mexico. This subchapter aims to shed light on the economic impacts of illegal immigration, which are often hotly debated. By analyzing various aspects such as job displacement, wage suppression, fiscal costs, and contributions to the economy, we can gain a comprehensive understanding of how this issue affects the economy of both nations.

Job Displacement and Wage Suppression:

One of the primary concerns surrounding illegal immigration is its potential to displace native workers and suppress wages. As undocumented immigrants often accept lower wages, they may compete with low-skilled American workers, leading to job losses and reduced wages in certain industries. This can be particularly detrimental to vulnerable populations already struggling to find employment.

Fiscal Costs and Contributions:

The fiscal impacts of illegal immigration are also crucial to consider. While undocumented immigrants may strain public resources such as education and healthcare, they also contribute to the economy through taxes and labor. Studies have shown that immigrants, including those without legal status, contribute billions of dollars in taxes each year. However, the overall net fiscal impact of illegal immigration remains a topic of ongoing debate.

Informal Economy and Entrepreneurship:

Illegal immigrants often find themselves working in the informal economy, which presents both challenges and opportunities. On one hand, this can lead to the exploitation of vulnerable workers and tax evasion. On the other hand, it can also foster entrepreneurship, as many undocumented immigrants start their own businesses, contributing to local economies and job creation.

Labor Market Flexibility and Economic Growth:

Illegal immigration can also have positive effects on the economy by providing labor market flexibility. Industries that heavily rely on low-skilled labor, such as agriculture and construction, benefit from the availability of a flexible workforce. This, in turn, can enhance economic growth and competitiveness.

Conclusion:

The economic impacts of illegal immigration are complex and multifaceted. While some argue that it negatively affects job opportunities and wages for native workers, others emphasize the contributions immigrants make to the economy through their labor and entrepreneurship. It is crucial for policymakers, legislators, and the public to have a nuanced understanding of these effects in order to develop effective and fair immigration policies that balance economic considerations with national security concerns. By addressing the root causes of illegal immigration and implementing comprehensive immigration reforms, it is possible to mitigate any negative economic impacts and harness the potential benefits that immigrants bring to our society.

Job Market Competition and Wage Suppression

In the ongoing debate surrounding the US-Mexico open border policy, one critical aspect that cannot be overlooked is the impact it has on the job market competition and wage suppression in the United States. This subchapter aims to shed light on the direct consequences of this policy on the American workforce and the overall economy.

The unrestricted flow of labor across the border undoubtedly increases competition for jobs in various sectors. With a large number of immigrants, both legal and illegal, entering the country, the labor market becomes saturated, putting downward pressure on wages. This means that American workers often find themselves competing with immigrants who are willing to accept lower wages, leading to wage suppression and reduced job opportunities for the native population.

Moreover, the presence of undocumented workers further exacerbates this issue. Employers often take advantage of their vulnerable status, paying them significantly lower wages and exploiting their labor. This not only hurts the wages of American workers but also creates an environment of unfair competition, where businesses can profit by paying substandard wages to undocumented workers.

The consequences of job market competition and wage suppression are far-reaching. Many Americans, particularly those in lower-skilled jobs, find it increasingly difficult to support themselves and their families due to the depressed wages. This, in turn, leads to a rise in poverty rates and an increased burden on social welfare programs.

Furthermore, the impact extends beyond individual workers. The suppressed wages have a ripple effect on the overall economy, leading to reduced consumer spending and slower economic growth. It also hampers innovation and productivity as businesses have less incentive to invest in their workforce or upgrade their operations.

Addressing these challenges requires a comprehensive approach that balances the need for a diverse labor force with the protection of American workers. Policymakers, legislators, and politicians must work together to develop responsible immigration policies that prioritize the interests of American workers while still recognizing the contributions that immigrants make to the economy.

In conclusion, the US-Mexico open border policy has significant implications for the job market competition and wage suppression in the United States. It is crucial for the public, politicians, and legislators to understand the consequences of this policy and work towards finding a balanced approach that benefits both American workers and immigrants. By addressing these issues, we can create a fair and prosperous job market that uplifts the American workforce and strengthens the overall economy.

Economic Policies to Mitigate Negative Impacts

Introduction:

The US-Mexico open border policy has significant economic implications that need to be carefully managed to mitigate any negative impacts. This subchapter focuses on the economic policies that can be implemented to address these concerns. It is crucial for the public, politicians, and legislators to understand the importance of effective economic policies in ensuring the security and stability of the border region.

1. Promoting Economic Development:

To counter the negative impacts of the open border policy, it is essential to prioritize economic development in border communities. This can be achieved by providing tax incentives and subsidies to attract businesses and create job opportunities. Additionally, investing in infrastructure, education, and training programs will enhance the region's workforce and increase its competitiveness.

2. Strengthening Border Security:

While economic development is crucial, it must be accompanied by robust border security measures. Allocating resources to enhance border patrol capabilities, deploying advanced surveillance technologies, and increasing personnel will help combat drug trafficking, human smuggling, and arms smuggling. By strengthening border security, the negative economic impacts associated with these criminal activities can be minimized.

3. Facilitating Legal Trade and Commerce:

Creating streamlined processes for legal trade and commerce is vital for the economic growth of both the US and Mexico. By reducing bureaucratic barriers, implementing efficient customs procedures, and harmonizing regulations, the flow of goods and services can be expedited, benefiting businesses on both sides of the border. This will stimulate economic activity and create job opportunities.

4. Investing in Public Health and Environmental Protection:

To address public health risks and environmental concerns, it is crucial to invest in disease control measures and wildlife conservation. Collaborative efforts between governments, NGOs, and local communities can help prevent the spread of diseases and protect the unique biodiversity of the border region. These investments will not only safeguard public health and the environment but also preserve the economic viability of the region.

Conclusion:

Implementing effective economic policies is vital to mitigate the negative impacts of the US-Mexico open border policy. By prioritizing economic development, strengthening border security, facilitating legal trade, and investing in public health and environmental protection, the economic stability and security of the border region can be ensured. It is imperative for politicians, legislators, and the public to recognize the importance of these policies to address the diverse challenges posed by the open border policy and foster a prosperous and secure future.

Chapter 8: Public Health Risks and Disease Control

Health Concerns Associated with Illegal Immigration

Introduction:

As the debate surrounding the US-Mexico open border policy rages on, it is crucial to address the various health concerns associated with illegal immigration. This subchapter aims to shed light on the potential risks posed by unregulated migration, emphasizing the importance of addressing these concerns for the well-being of the public and the nation.

Public Health Risks:

One of the primary concerns associated with illegal immigration is the potential for the spread of infectious diseases. As individuals cross the border without proper health screenings, they may unknowingly introduce diseases into the host country. This poses a significant risk to public health, as these diseases can rapidly spread throughout communities, overwhelming healthcare systems and endangering the population at large.

Limited Access to Healthcare:

Illegal immigrants often face numerous barriers to accessing healthcare, including financial constraints and fear of deportation. This lack of access not only puts their own health at risk but also increases the likelihood of contagious diseases going untreated. Consequently, this can lead to outbreaks that affect both immigrant communities and the general public, placing additional strain on already stretched healthcare resources.

Impact on Local Communities:

The influx of illegal immigrants can place a burden on local communities, particularly in regions with limited healthcare infrastructure. Local hospitals, clinics, and schools may struggle to meet the increased demand, resulting in longer waiting times, overcrowding, and reduced quality of care for both immigrants and citizens. This strain on resources can lead to a decline in overall public health standards, affecting everyone in the region.

Addressing the Concerns:

To mitigate the health concerns associated with illegal immigration, a comprehensive approach is required. This includes implementing robust health screening protocols at the border, ensuring all individuals entering the country undergo thorough examinations. Additionally, providing accessible and affordable healthcare options for immigrants can help prevent the spread of diseases and ensure early detection and treatment.

Collaboration between government agencies, healthcare providers, and community organizations is essential to develop strategies that address these concerns effectively. By working together, we can safeguard public health, protect communities, and create a more secure and prosperous nation.

Conclusion:

Health concerns associated with illegal immigration are a pressing issue that must be acknowledged and addressed by policymakers, legislators, and the public. By focusing on the risks posed by unregulated migration, we can develop comprehensive strategies to protect public health, mitigate the spread of infectious diseases, and provide adequate healthcare access for all. Effective border security measures that prioritize health screenings and collaboration between relevant stakeholders are vital in achieving these objectives. Only by addressing these concerns can we ensure the well-being of our communities and uphold the integrity of our nation's healthcare system.

Disease Spread and Control Measures

Introduction:

The issue of disease spread and control along the US-Mexico border is a critical concern that affects not only the public but also politicians and legislators. This subchapter aims to shed light on the challenges posed by the open border policy and proposes measures for effective disease control. It is imperative that we address this issue as part of our overall approach to homeland security threats.

The Threat:

The US-Mexico open border policy presents unique challenges in terms of disease spread. With the movement of people across the border, there is an increased risk of infectious diseases entering both countries. This poses a significant threat to public health and necessitates immediate attention.

Control Measures:

1. Enhanced Border Screening: Implementing rigorous health screenings at border checkpoints can help identify individuals with contagious diseases. This includes temperature checks, medical questionnaires, and rapid diagnostic tests. Suspected cases should be isolated and provided with necessary medical care.

2. Strengthened Disease Surveillance: Establishing a comprehensive disease surveillance system is crucial for early detection and response. This includes sharing information between medical facilities on both sides of the border, monitoring disease outbreaks, and conducting joint investigations to identify the source of infections.

3. Vaccination Programs: Promote and facilitate vaccination campaigns on both sides of the border to ensure that people are protected against common infectious diseases. This will not only reduce the risk of disease spread but also improve overall public health.

4. Collaboration and Information Sharing: Enhance cooperation between US and Mexican health authorities to share information, expertise, and resources. This includes joint training programs for healthcare professionals, cross-border research collaborations, and sharing best practices in disease control.

5. Public Health Education: Conduct awareness campaigns to educate the public about the risks of disease spread and the importance of preventive measures. This includes promoting hygiene practices, such as handwashing and proper sanitation, and educating individuals on the symptoms and transmission of contagious diseases.

Conclusion:

Addressing the public health risks associated with disease spread due to the US-Mexico open border policy is crucial for the overall security and well-being of both nations. By implementing these control measures, we can minimize the threat of infectious diseases and protect the health of our citizens. It is imperative that politicians, legislators, and the public come together to address this issue and ensure a safer and healthier future for all.

Addressing Public Health Challenges at the Border

The US-Mexico open border policy has undoubtedly brought a myriad of challenges to both nations, one of the most pressing being public health risks and disease control. The movement of people across the border has the potential to facilitate the spread of infectious diseases, posing a significant threat to public health.

The proximity of the border has made it easier for communicable diseases to cross over, including tuberculosis, influenza, and sexually transmitted infections. The lack of proper screening measures and limited access to healthcare services for undocumented immigrants exacerbate the situation. As a result, these diseases can quickly spread within border communities and beyond, endangering the health of both Americans and Mexicans.

To effectively address these public health challenges, it is crucial for policymakers, politicians, and legislators to prioritize the development and implementation of comprehensive strategies. Firstly, investing in adequate healthcare infrastructure along the border is essential. This includes increasing the number of healthcare facilities, clinics, and hospitals, as well as ensuring sufficient medical personnel to cater to the needs of both local residents and migrants.

Additionally, there must be a focus on enhancing disease surveillance and early detection systems. This involves collaborating with both the Mexican and American health authorities to share information and coordinate efforts in monitoring and responding to outbreaks. Regular health screenings at the border checkpoints, including testing for infectious diseases, should be mandatory to prevent the entry and spread of diseases.

Another critical aspect is the promotion of public health education and awareness campaigns. This includes disseminating information about preventive measures, such as vaccination campaigns and safe practices to minimize the risk of disease transmission. Targeted education programs should be developed to reach vulnerable populations, such as migrants and border communities.

Furthermore, cross-border collaborations in research and development are vital to finding effective solutions to public health challenges. By fostering partnerships between universities, research institutions, and healthcare providers on both sides of the border, innovative approaches can be developed to address specific health issues prevalent in border regions.

In conclusion, addressing public health challenges at the US-Mexico border requires a multi-faceted approach that encompasses infrastructure development, disease surveillance, public health education, and cross-border collaborations. By prioritizing these strategies, we can mitigate the risks posed by infectious diseases and protect the health and well-being of both border communities and the wider population.

Chapter 9: Environmental Concerns and Wildlife Trafficking

Impact of Border Activities on the Environment

The impact of border activities on the environment is a critical aspect that needs to be addressed when discussing the US-Mexico open border policy. The border region is home to diverse ecosystems, wildlife, and natural resources that are at risk due to various factors associated with border activities.

One significant environmental concern is the destruction of habitats and ecosystems caused by drug trafficking and cartel violence. These criminal activities often involve the construction of illegal roads and tunnels, leading to deforestation, soil erosion, and degradation of sensitive areas. Additionally, the use of chemicals in drug production and cultivation has severe consequences for local flora and fauna, poisoning water sources and disrupting the ecological balance.

Human smuggling and trafficking also have a detrimental impact on the environment. The large influx of people crossing the border illegally leads to increased pressure on fragile ecosystems, resulting in soil erosion, pollution, and habitat destruction. In many cases, migrants resort to illegal logging, hunting, and fishing to sustain themselves during their journey, further exacerbating environmental degradation.

Terrorism and border security have their own set of environmental concerns. The construction of border walls, fences, and surveillance infrastructure can disrupt natural migration patterns of wildlife and disrupt their habitats. Additionally, the increased militarization of the border can result in the displacement of endangered species and disrupt fragile ecosystems.

Arms smuggling and the illegal firearms trade pose significant risks to the environment. The trafficking of weapons often leads to an increase in violence and poaching, threatening endangered species and disrupting ecosystems. The illegal use of firearms can also result in the indiscriminate killing of animals and destruction of natural resources.

Furthermore, the economic impacts and job displacement associated with border activities can indirectly harm the environment. As individuals seek employment opportunities in border regions, urbanization and infrastructure development can lead to the destruction of natural habitats and increased pollution levels.

It is crucial to address these environmental concerns and implement policies that promote sustainable border management. This includes investing in technologies and strategies that minimize the ecological footprint of border activities, such as employing drones for surveillance instead of constructing physical barriers. Additionally, collaboration between border agencies and environmental organizations can help mitigate the environmental impacts of border activities through initiatives focused on conservation, habitat restoration, and sustainable resource management.

By considering the environmental consequences of border activities, we can strive to strike a balance between national security and environmental stewardship. This requires the cooperation and support of the public, politicians, and legislators in implementing policies that prioritize the protection of our shared natural heritage. Only through collective efforts can we ensure a secure border that does not come at the expense of our environment.

Wildlife Trafficking and Endangered Species

One of the lesser-known but equally critical consequences of the US-Mexico open border policy is the rampant wildlife trafficking and the devastating impact it has on endangered species. This subchapter aims to shed light on this pressing issue, bringing it to the attention of the public, politicians, and legislators.

Wildlife trafficking is a highly lucrative and illegal trade that involves the smuggling and sale of endangered species and their parts. The US-Mexico border serves as a major gateway for this illicit trade, with countless species falling victim to this nefarious activity. From elephants and rhinos to tigers and pangolins, the list of endangered species targeted by wildlife traffickers is vast.

The consequences of wildlife trafficking are far-reaching and multifaceted. First and foremost, it poses a severe threat to biodiversity and the delicate balance of ecosystems. By removing key species from their natural habitats, wildlife trafficking disrupts the intricate web of life, leading to potential ecosystem collapse and the loss of critical ecological services.

Furthermore, wildlife trafficking has significant economic consequences. The demand for exotic pets, traditional medicine ingredients, and luxury goods made from animal parts fuels a black market economy that siphons billions of dollars away from legitimate industries. This illicit trade not only undermines local economies but also perpetuates corruption and organized crime, further exacerbating the challenges faced by border security officials.

From a public health perspective, wildlife trafficking also poses significant risks. Many of the animals traded illegally carry zoonotic diseases, which can easily be transmitted to humans. Diseases such as Ebola, SARS, and COVID-19 have all been linked to the wildlife trade, highlighting the need for robust disease control measures and strict border management.

Addressing wildlife trafficking requires a multi-faceted approach that encompasses legislation, law enforcement, education, and international cooperation. Stricter border controls, increased penalties for offenders, and public awareness campaigns can all contribute to curbing this illicit trade. Collaborative efforts between the US and Mexico, as well as international organizations, are vital to effectively combat wildlife trafficking and protect endangered species.

In conclusion, wildlife trafficking and the endangerment of species is a pressing issue that demands immediate attention. By understanding the devastating consequences of this illicit trade, the public, politicians, and legislators can work together to strengthen border security, enact meaningful legislation, and protect the irreplaceable wildlife that inhabits our planet.

Conservation Efforts and Border Management

Conservation efforts and border management are crucial aspects of addressing the homeland security threats posed by the US-Mexico open border policy. This subchapter will shed light on the importance of protecting the environment, managing wildlife trafficking, and implementing effective border infrastructure to ensure the safety and security of both nations.

The US-Mexico border region is home to diverse ecosystems and rich biodiversity. However, the unchecked flow of people, drugs, and weapons across the border poses significant risks to the environment. Conservation efforts are essential to mitigate these risks and preserve the delicate balance of ecosystems. By implementing measures such as increased patrol and surveillance, habitat restoration, and cooperation between border agencies, we can minimize the negative impacts on the environment.

Wildlife trafficking is another critical issue directly linked to border security. The US-Mexico border serves as a major transit route for illegal wildlife trade, endangering many species and disrupting fragile ecosystems. Strengthening border management and implementing strict penalties for wildlife trafficking can help curb this problem. Additionally, public awareness campaigns can educate people about the consequences of buying and selling illegal wildlife products, reducing the demand for such activities.

Effective border infrastructure and management are essential for maintaining national security. The US-Mexico border is vast and challenging to monitor, making it easier for criminals and terrorists to exploit its vulnerabilities. By investing in advanced technology, such as drones, sensors, and surveillance systems, we can enhance border security and detect illegal activities more efficiently. Moreover, increasing the number of border patrol agents and providing them with proper training and resources is crucial for effective border management.

The public, politicians, and legislators must recognize the interconnectedness of conservation efforts and border management with homeland security. By addressing issues such as drug trafficking, cartel violence, human smuggling, terrorism, arms smuggling, economic impacts, public health risks, and cybersecurity threats, we can create a comprehensive approach to border security. Cooperation between the United States and Mexico, as well as international organizations, is crucial for the success of these efforts.

In conclusion, conservation efforts and effective border management play a vital role in addressing the homeland security threats posed by the US-Mexico open border policy. By protecting the environment, combating wildlife trafficking, and implementing advanced border infrastructure, we can ensure the safety and security of both nations. It is imperative that the public, politicians, and legislators understand the importance of these measures and work together to address the multifaceted challenges associated with border insecurity.

Chapter 10: Border Infrastructure and Management Challenges

Overview of Border Infrastructure

The US-Mexico border is a complex and vast region that spans over 1,900 miles, presenting unique challenges and threats that require careful attention. The infrastructure and management of this border play a crucial role in addressing the homeland security threats posed by the open border policy between the two nations. This subchapter aims to provide an overview of the key aspects related to border infrastructure and management challenges.

Border infrastructure refers to the physical structures, systems, and technologies in place to regulate and control the flow of goods, people, and information across the border. It includes ports of entry, border checkpoints, surveillance systems, communication networks, and transportation infrastructure. The effectiveness of these infrastructure components is essential in ensuring the security and integrity of the border.

One of the primary concerns regarding border infrastructure is drug trafficking and cartel violence. The US-Mexico border has been a major route for drug smuggling, with cartels exploiting the vulnerabilities in border infrastructure to transport illicit narcotics. Strengthening and enhancing border infrastructure can help disrupt these activities, improving drug interdiction efforts and reducing the violence associated with drug cartels.

Another critical aspect of border infrastructure is the management of human smuggling and trafficking. The open border policy has made it easier for criminal organizations to exploit vulnerable individuals and engage in human trafficking. By implementing robust border infrastructure, such as biometric systems and improved surveillance capabilities, authorities can better detect and prevent these illicit activities, ensuring the safety and well-being of individuals attempting to cross the border.

Terrorism and border security are also significant concerns that must be addressed through effective border infrastructure. The porous nature of the US-Mexico border presents an opportunity for terrorists to infiltrate the country and carry out attacks. By investing in advanced technologies, intelligence sharing, and enhanced border surveillance, the risk of terrorist activities can be mitigated, safeguarding national security.

Additionally, border infrastructure plays a crucial role in combating arms smuggling and the illegal firearms trade. The border is a primary gateway for the illegal movement of firearms, posing a significant threat to public safety. By implementing strict border controls, increasing law enforcement presence, and deploying advanced detection technologies, the flow of illegal arms can be curbed, reducing violence and crime rates.

Moreover, border infrastructure has economic implications, including job displacement and impacts on local communities. The open border policy can lead to unfair competition, job losses, and economic imbalances. Properly managed border infrastructure can facilitate legitimate trade and commerce while protecting domestic industries and ensuring fair employment practices.

Public health risks and disease control are also vital considerations in border infrastructure planning. The movement of people across the border can pose challenges in preventing the spread of infectious diseases. Adequate infrastructure, such as healthcare screening facilities and quarantine measures, can help mitigate these risks, protecting public health on both sides of the border.

Environmental concerns and wildlife trafficking are additional issues that require attention in border infrastructure planning. The border region is known for its rich biodiversity and fragile ecosystems. Properly designed infrastructure can minimize the impact on the environment, while also addressing wildlife trafficking and illegal trade in endangered species.

In conclusion, border infrastructure and management challenges are critical aspects of addressing the homeland security threats posed by the US-Mexico open border policy. By investing in advanced technologies, strengthening border controls, and improving communication and coordination between relevant agencies, the risks associated with drug trafficking, human smuggling, terrorism, arms smuggling, and other criminal activities can be effectively mitigated. Moreover, border infrastructure can ensure the economic well-being, public health, environmental conservation, and overall security of both nations.

Challenges in Border Management and Surveillance

Border management and surveillance are crucial aspects of maintaining national security and protecting the interests of any country. In the case of the US-Mexico open border policy, numerous challenges arise that demand immediate attention and effective solutions. This subchapter aims to shed light on the key challenges faced in border management and surveillance, providing valuable insights for the public, politicians, and legislators.

One of the greatest threats posed by an open border policy is drug trafficking and cartel violence. The porous border allows drug cartels to smuggle illegal drugs into the United States, fueling addiction, crime, and violence. Effective border management and surveillance strategies are needed to detect and intercept drug smuggling operations, dismantle criminal networks, and disrupt the flow of illicit substances.

Human smuggling and trafficking is another pressing concern. The open border provides opportunities for human traffickers to exploit vulnerable individuals, subjecting them to forced labor, prostitution, and other forms of exploitation. Enhancing border management and surveillance capabilities is crucial to identifying and rescuing victims, apprehending traffickers, and preventing further human rights abuses.

The threat of terrorism is a significant concern when it comes to border security. An open border policy creates vulnerabilities that can be exploited by terrorists seeking entry into the United States. Strengthening border management and surveillance efforts is essential to identifying potential threats, preventing terrorist activities, and safeguarding national security.

Arms smuggling and the illegal firearms trade are also challenges that must be addressed. The open border facilitates the movement of illegal weapons, contributing to the proliferation of violence and crime. Implementing robust border management and surveillance measures can help intercept illegal firearms, disrupt arms smuggling networks, and reduce the availability of weapons in the wrong hands.

The economic impacts and job displacement caused by an open border policy cannot be overlooked. Unregulated migration can strain local economies, leading to job losses and increased competition for limited resources. Effective border management and surveillance strategies are necessary to ensure a controlled and orderly flow of people and resources, mitigating the negative economic consequences.

Public health risks and disease control are additional concerns associated with open borders. Unregulated migration can introduce infectious diseases, putting public health at risk. Strengthening border management and surveillance is vital in implementing health screenings, quarantine measures, and disease control protocols to protect public health.

Environmental concerns and wildlife trafficking also pose significant challenges. The open border policy can lead to illegal wildlife trade and environmental degradation. Comprehensive border management and surveillance efforts are necessary to combat wildlife trafficking, protect endangered species, and preserve natural habitats.

Border infrastructure and management challenges must be addressed to ensure the effective implementation of border management and surveillance strategies. Adequate resources, technology, and personnel are required to manage the vast border efficiently.

Cybersecurity threats and digital crime are emerging challenges in border management and surveillance. As technology advances, criminals exploit digital platforms for illicit activities. Strengthening cybersecurity measures and enhancing digital crime detection capabilities are imperative to safeguard national security.

Lastly, border corruption and organized crime infiltration demand attention. Criminal elements may attempt to infiltrate border security agencies, compromising the effectiveness of border management and surveillance. Implementing stringent anti-corruption measures and enhancing cooperation between law enforcement agencies are crucial to combating organized crime and maintaining border integrity.

In conclusion, effective border management and surveillance are critical to addressing the numerous challenges associated with an open border policy between the US and Mexico. By understanding and tackling these challenges, policymakers, legislators, and the public can work together to ensure the security, prosperity, and well-being of both nations.

Improving Border Infrastructure and Operations

Introduction:

The US-Mexico open border policy has long been a contentious issue, raising concerns about homeland security threats, drug trafficking, human smuggling, terrorism, arms smuggling, economic impacts, public health risks, environmental concerns, border infrastructure challenges, cybersecurity threats, and border corruption. This subchapter will delve into the importance of improving border infrastructure and operations to address these pressing issues and ensure the safety and well-being of the public.

Enhancing Border Infrastructure:

One of the key aspects of improving border security is investing in robust and modern infrastructure. This includes constructing physical barriers, expanding and upgrading ports of entry, deploying advanced surveillance technologies, and implementing efficient transportation systems. By strengthening the physical border, we can deter unauthorized crossings, enhance law enforcement capabilities, and facilitate legitimate trade and travel while preventing illicit activities.

Streamlining Border Operations:

In addition to infrastructure improvement, optimizing border operations is crucial for effective security. This involves enhancing coordination and collaboration among various agencies responsible for border management, such as Customs and Border Protection (CBP), Immigration and Customs Enforcement (ICE), and local law enforcement. By establishing integrated databases, utilizing data analytics, and implementing risk-based screening procedures, we can identify and intercept potential threats more efficiently, while minimizing disruptions to legitimate border crossings.

Investing in Technology and Innovation:

Advancements in technology play a vital role in border security. The development and deployment of state-of-the-art technologies, such as drones, biometric systems, artificial intelligence, and predictive analytics, can significantly enhance surveillance, intelligence gathering, and threat assessment capabilities. Additionally, investing in research and development can lead to innovative solutions to counter emerging threats, such as cyberattacks and digital crimes that exploit vulnerabilities in our interconnected world.

Promoting International Cooperation:

Addressing border security threats requires collaboration with our neighbors and international partners. Strengthening diplomatic ties and engaging in joint operations, intelligence sharing, and training programs can improve information exchange, target transnational criminal organizations, and disrupt illicit networks. By fostering international cooperation, we can create a united front against drug trafficking, human smuggling, terrorism, and other threats that transcend national borders.

Conclusion:

Improving border infrastructure and operations is crucial to tackling the various homeland security threats associated with the US-Mexico open border policy. By investing in modern infrastructure, streamlining operations, embracing technology and innovation, and promoting international cooperation, we can enhance border security, protect public safety, and safeguard the economic and environmental well-being of our nation. It is imperative that politicians, legislators, and the public recognize the importance of these improvements and work together to address the complex challenges posed by the US-Mexico border.

Chapter 11: Cybersecurity Threats and Digital Crime

Cyber Threats Targeting Border Security

In today's interconnected world, cyber threats pose a significant challenge to border security. As technology advances, so do the tactics of criminals and terrorist organizations seeking to exploit vulnerabilities in border control systems. This subchapter aims to shed light on the cyber threats targeting border security, their implications, and the urgent need for effective cybersecurity measures.

One of the primary cyber threats facing border security is the hacking of critical infrastructure systems. Border control agencies heavily rely on technology to monitor and manage border crossings, from surveillance cameras to facial recognition systems. However, these systems are susceptible to cyber-attacks that can disrupt operations, compromise sensitive data, or even allow unauthorized access into the country. Such attacks could have severe consequences, including the infiltration of terrorists or the smuggling of contraband.

Another growing concern is the use of cyber tactics by criminal organizations involved in drug trafficking and cartel violence. These groups have been quick to exploit the anonymity of the internet to coordinate their operations, communicate with associates, and launder money. Moreover, they frequently use advanced hacking techniques to breach border control systems, enabling the smuggling of drugs across the border undetected. These cyber-enabled activities pose a significant threat to both public safety and national security.

Terrorist organizations are also utilizing cyberspace to further their agendas and target border security. From spreading propaganda and recruiting followers to planning attacks and fundraising, terrorist networks have embraced the digital realm. Cyber-attacks on border control systems can be part of their strategy to weaken security measures and create opportunities for infiltration. As such, it is crucial to prioritize cybersecurity in efforts to counter terrorism and maintain border integrity.

The issue of cyber threats targeting border security extends beyond criminal activities. Arms smuggling and illegal firearms trade have increasingly found a home in the dark corners of the internet. Online platforms provide a convenient avenue for the sale and distribution of illicit weapons, circumventing traditional border control measures. Cybersecurity measures must address this threat to prevent these dangerous weapons from reaching the wrong hands.

In conclusion, cyber threats pose a significant challenge to border security, necessitating urgent attention and robust cybersecurity measures. The hacking of critical infrastructure systems, the use of cyber tactics by criminal and terrorist organizations, the facilitation of arms smuggling, and the exploitation of digital platforms all contribute to the vulnerability of border control systems. To effectively address these threats, it is crucial for the public, politicians, and legislators to recognize the importance of investing in cybersecurity, enhancing collaboration between agencies, and staying ahead of evolving cyber threats. Only through a comprehensive and proactive approach can we ensure the integrity and security of our borders.

Digital Crime and Identity Theft

In this subchapter, we will delve into the pressing issue of digital crime and identity theft that has emerged as a significant concern within the context of the US-Mexico open border policy. As technology continues to advance at an unprecedented rate, so do the methods employed by criminals to exploit vulnerabilities and wreak havoc on individuals, organizations, and even nations.

The border region between the United States and Mexico has become a hotbed for digital crime due to its unique characteristics. The open border policy has inadvertently created opportunities for criminals to engage in cyber activities, such as hacking, phishing, and identity theft. These crimes transcend geographical boundaries and can be perpetrated from anywhere in the world, making them difficult to tackle effectively.

Identity theft, in particular, has become a rampant problem in the border region. Criminals steal personal information, such as social security numbers, credit card details, and bank account information, to assume false identities and commit fraudulent activities. The consequences of identity theft can be devastating for individuals who may find themselves financially ruined and struggling to regain control over their lives.

Moreover, digital crime poses a significant threat to national security. Cybercriminals can target critical infrastructure, government databases, and even military systems, potentially causing disruption and compromising sensitive information. With the open border policy, the risk of cyberattacks from foreign entities becomes even more pronounced.

To address these challenges, it is imperative for policymakers, legislators, and the public to recognize the gravity of digital crime and identity theft. Adequate funding and resources must be allocated to law enforcement agencies and cybersecurity initiatives to enhance their capabilities in detecting, preventing, and prosecuting cybercriminals.

Furthermore, public awareness campaigns should be conducted to educate individuals about the importance of safeguarding their personal information, recognizing potential scams, and adopting strong cybersecurity practices. This can include using complex passwords, regularly updating software, and being cautious when sharing personal information online.

Collaboration between the United States and Mexico is of utmost importance in combating digital crime and identity theft. Cross-border partnerships should be established to facilitate information sharing, joint investigations, and the development of comprehensive cybersecurity strategies.

In conclusion, digital crime and identity theft pose significant threats within the context of the US-Mexico open border policy. The ever-evolving nature of technology necessitates a proactive approach to combat these crimes effectively. By prioritizing cybersecurity, promoting public awareness, and fostering international collaboration, we can strive to minimize the risks associated with digital crime and protect the interests of individuals, organizations, and nations alike.

Enhancing Cybersecurity Measures and Collaboration

In recent years, as the world becomes increasingly interconnected through digital platforms, the importance of cybersecurity cannot be overstated. This is especially true in the context of the US-Mexico open border policy, where the risks and challenges associated with cyber threats are becoming more prevalent. As such, it is crucial for policymakers, legislators, and the public to prioritize enhancing cybersecurity measures and collaboration to safeguard the interests of both nations.

The rapid advancement of technology has provided criminals and malicious actors with new avenues to exploit vulnerabilities and infiltrate systems. As we witness an alarming increase in cybercrimes targeting not only government institutions but also critical infrastructure, it is imperative that comprehensive cybersecurity measures are put in place. This includes robust firewalls, advanced encryption techniques, and the constant monitoring of networks to detect and mitigate potential threats.

Collaboration between the United States and Mexico is pivotal in addressing these cybersecurity challenges. Both countries must work together to share information, intelligence, and best practices to enhance their respective cybersecurity capabilities. This collaboration should extend beyond government agencies to include private sector entities, academia, and cybersecurity experts. By pooling resources and expertise, a stronger defense against cyber threats can be established.

Furthermore, public awareness and education play a significant role in enhancing cybersecurity measures. Individuals should be educated about the risks associated with cybercrimes and be taught how to protect themselves online. This can be achieved through public awareness campaigns, workshops, and the incorporation of cybersecurity education in school curricula. Additionally, promoting a culture of reporting cybercrimes and encouraging citizens to report suspicious activities can help in the early detection and prevention of cyber threats.

It is important to recognize that cyber threats do not respect borders. Therefore, international frameworks and agreements should be developed to facilitate collaboration and information sharing between nations. Such agreements should address jurisdictional challenges, promote data protection and privacy, and establish a framework for the prosecution of cybercriminals.

In conclusion, enhancing cybersecurity measures and collaboration is of paramount importance in the context of the US-Mexico open border policy. By investing in robust cybersecurity infrastructure, fostering collaboration between nations, promoting public awareness, and establishing international frameworks, we can effectively combat cyber threats and protect the interests of both countries. This requires the collective effort of the public, politicians, legislators, and stakeholders from various niches, as cybersecurity is a shared responsibility that demands a united front.

Chapter 12: Border Corruption and Organized Crime Infiltration

Corruption Challenges at the Border

Introduction:

The issue of corruption at the US-Mexico border is a critical concern that demands immediate attention. This subchapter aims to shed light on the various corruption challenges faced at the border, highlighting their detrimental impact on homeland security, public safety, and the overall well-being of both nations. By addressing these issues, we hope to raise awareness among the public, politicians, and legislators, urging them to take action and implement effective measures to combat corruption.

The Nexus of Corruption and Border Security:

Corruption poses a significant threat to border security as it undermines the integrity of law enforcement agencies and compromises their ability to effectively enforce immigration and customs laws. This subchapter will explore how corrupt practices, such as bribery, collusion, and money laundering, enable criminal organizations to exploit vulnerabilities in the border control system.

Impacts on Drug Trafficking and Cartel Violence:

Corruption at the border directly contributes to the flourishing drug trade and cartel violence. We will delve into how corrupt officials facilitate drug trafficking by turning a blind eye to illegal activities, aiding cartels in their operations, and receiving bribes in return. By exposing these practices, we aim to emphasize the urgent need for comprehensive anti-corruption measures to disrupt the drug trade and reduce violence.

Human Smuggling and Trafficking:

Corruption also plays a significant role in human smuggling and trafficking networks. This subchapter will explore how corrupt officials facilitate the movement of undocumented migrants and enable the exploitation of vulnerable individuals. By highlighting these practices, we aim to advocate for stronger border controls, enhanced training for law enforcement personnel, and increased cooperation between relevant agencies to combat these grave human rights violations.

Terrorism and Border Security:

Corruption at the border poses a significant risk to national security by potentially allowing terrorists to exploit weak points in the system. We will discuss how corrupt officials may be manipulated or compromised by terrorist organizations, compromising the safety of both nations. This subchapter will underscore the importance of robust anti-corruption measures and intelligence-sharing initiatives to secure the border against potential terrorist threats.

Conclusion:

The challenges posed by corruption at the US-Mexico border cannot be overlooked. This subchapter seeks to raise awareness among the public, politicians, and legislators about the detrimental impacts of corruption on various aspects of border security. By understanding the gravity of the situation, we hope to encourage the implementation of effective anti-corruption strategies, collaboration between law enforcement agencies, and the allocation of adequate resources to safeguard our borders and protect our nations from the threats posed by corruption and organized crime infiltration.

Infiltration of Organized Crime Groups

The infiltration of organized crime groups is a grave concern that must be addressed when discussing the homeland security threats posed by the US-Mexico open border policy. These criminal organizations, such as drug cartels and human trafficking rings, exploit the vulnerabilities of our border to carry out their illicit activities, posing a significant risk to our society.

One of the most prominent issues stemming from the infiltration of organized crime groups is drug trafficking and cartel violence. These criminal organizations utilize the open border to transport illegal drugs, such as cocaine, heroin, and methamphetamine, into the United States. The consequences of this illicit trade are devastating, fueling addiction, violence, and the degradation of communities on both sides of the border.

Moreover, the infiltration of organized crime groups enables the proliferation of human smuggling and trafficking networks. These criminal enterprises exploit vulnerable individuals, often exposing them to extreme risks and inhumane conditions. By infiltrating our border, these groups continue to profit from the desperation and suffering of countless people seeking a better life.

Terrorism is another significant concern linked to the infiltration of organized crime groups. The porous border allows potential terrorists to exploit the weaknesses in our security infrastructure, making it easier for them to enter the country undetected. This poses a grave threat to national security and necessitates a comprehensive approach to border security.

Furthermore, the infiltration of organized crime groups facilitates the illegal arms trade, contributing to the proliferation of firearms in our communities. These weapons end up in the hands of criminals, exacerbating violence and posing a threat to public safety. It is imperative that we strengthen our border security measures to prevent the smuggling of illegal firearms.

The economic impacts of organized crime infiltration cannot be overlooked either. These criminal networks infiltrate legitimate businesses, engaging in money laundering and other illicit activities that undermine our economy. Additionally, job displacement occurs as legal businesses struggle to compete with the black market activities of these criminal organizations.

In conclusion, the infiltration of organized crime groups presents an array of homeland security threats that must be addressed urgently. From drug trafficking and cartel violence to human smuggling and trafficking, terrorism, arms smuggling, and economic impacts, the dangers are manifold. It is crucial that the public, politicians, and legislators understand the gravity of these threats and work together to develop comprehensive border security measures to combat the infiltration of organized crime groups effectively. Only by doing so can we safeguard our communities, protect our citizens, and preserve the integrity of our nation.

Strategies to Combat Border Corruption and Organized Crime

Introduction:

Border corruption and the infiltration of organized crime pose significant threats to the security and well-being of both the United States and Mexico. This subchapter will outline several strategies that can be implemented to address these challenges effectively. By targeting the root causes of corruption and organized crime, we can enhance border security and safeguard our communities.

1. Strengthening Law Enforcement:

One of the foremost strategies to combat border corruption and organized crime is to bolster the capabilities of law enforcement agencies. This involves providing adequate resources, technology, and training to border patrol agents, customs officers, and other relevant personnel.

Additionally, establishing a strong network of intelligence sharing and cooperation between US and Mexican law enforcement agencies is crucial for effective border security.

2. Implementing Transparent and Accountable Procedures:

To combat corruption, it is vital to establish transparent and accountable procedures at the border. This includes strict protocols for hiring, vetting, and promoting personnel involved in border security. Regular audits and inspections can also be conducted to identify and address any potential instances of corruption. By promoting integrity and accountability, we can minimize the opportunities for criminal infiltration.

3. Enhancing Cross-Border Cooperation:

Close collaboration between the US and Mexican governments is essential to combatting organized crime. Joint task forces, intelligence sharing, and coordinated operations can help dismantle criminal networks that exploit the border. Additionally, implementing bilateral agreements and extradition treaties can facilitate the prosecution and punishment of individuals involved in cross-border criminal activities.

4. Utilizing Technology and Surveillance:

Investing in advanced technology and surveillance systems can significantly enhance border security. Utilizing drones, sensors, and other monitoring devices can help detect and prevent illegal activities such as drug trafficking, human smuggling, and arms smuggling. Moreover, implementing biometric systems at border checkpoints can enhance identity verification and reduce the risk of corruption.

5. Public Awareness and Education:

Raising public awareness about the detrimental impacts of border corruption and organized crime is crucial. Educating the public, politicians, and legislators about the consequences of these threats can generate support for robust border security measures. Additionally, campaigns emphasizing the importance of reporting any suspicious activities can help in identifying and preventing criminal infiltration.

Conclusion:

Addressing the challenges of border corruption and organized crime requires a multifaceted approach involving law enforcement, cross-border cooperation, technology, public awareness, and accountable procedures. By implementing these strategies, we can strengthen border security, protect our communities, and uphold the values of justice and integrity. It is imperative that the public, politicians, and legislators come together to support these efforts and foster a safer and more secure border region.